WHAT'S IT LIKE TO BE A

BABY LION?

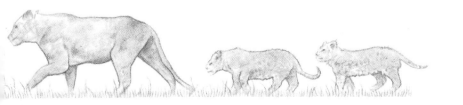

First published in the UK in 1998 by

Belitha Press Limited,
London House, Great Eastern Wharf,
Parkgate Road, London SW11 4NQ

This paperback edition first published in 1999

Editor Honor Head
Designer Hayley Cove
Illustrator Matthew Nicholas
Picture research Diana Morris
Consultants Sally Morgan and Wendy Body

ISBN 1 85561 852 4 (paperback)
ISBN 1 85561 764 1 (hardback)

Cataloguing in Publication Data for this book
is available from the British Library

Printed in Hong Kong / China

Photo credits
Daniel J. Cox/Getty Images: 29b.
Tim Davis/Getty Images: 30.
Eichorn/Zingel/FLPA: 21t.
Gerry Ellis/BBC Natural History Unit: 29t.
David Hosking/FLPA: 24t.
M. & C. Denis-Huot/Planet Earth Pictures: 6.
David Keith Jones/Images of Africa: 4, 18.
Renee Lynn/Getty Images: 13.
Mark Newman/FLPA: 11, 15, 19, 23.
Mark Petersen/Getty Images: 14.
Jonathan Scott/Planet Earth Pictures: 8, 10,
    16-17, 17t.
Anup Shah/BBC Natural History Unit: front
    cover, 22.
Roger Tidman/NHPA: 24b.
W. Wisniewski/FLPA: 21b, 26.
Gunter Ziesler/Bruce Coleman Ltd: 27.

WHAT'S IT LIKE TO BE A
BABY LION?

by Honor Head

Illustrated by
Matthew Nicholas

 Belitha Press

Lions live in a large family group. They live in Africa and parts of India where it is very hot.

Baby lions are called cubs. This book will tell you what it is like to be a cub.

When you read
this book imagine
that you are
a baby lion...

You are born in a
safe hiding place
away from the family.
When you are born
you are tiny. You
cannot see and
you cannot walk.

You have one or two brothers or sisters born at the same time. You open your eyes a few days after you are born.

Your eyes are a light grey-blue colour at first. They will turn to a light brown colour over the next few months.

You learn to walk when
you are about three
weeks old. Until you can
walk your mother carries
you from place to place
in her mouth.

She moves you from one hiding place to another at least once a week to keep you safe.

After about six weeks your mother takes you to join the rest of the family group.

When you are a cub you have a fluffy, spotted coat. As you grow, the markings fade away.

Your short tail will grow until it is quite long. It will have a little tuft of black hair on the end.

You have big, floppy paws
with soft pads on the
bottom and claws like
needles. You use the
rough bark of trees to
sharpen your claws.

You live in a group called a pride. It will have about three adult males and six females. There will be other cubs of all ages.

The lionesses hunt for food together while the males stay behind to protect you and the other cubs from enemies.

You are very playful.
You love to play fighting
and hunting games.

You chase the other
cubs. You pretend you
are hunting for food.

You play with a long twig and pretend it is food you have caught.

Usually all the lionesses have their babies at the same time. This means you have lots of other cubs to play with.

You purr when you are happy and make little squealing noises. When you get older you will be able to roar loudly and growl.

When your mother wants you to follow her, she grunts softly.

When she snarls at you and shows her teeth, it means she wants some peace and quiet.

You sleep for most of the day. You sleep on the ground or sometimes in the trees so that you do not get bitten by insects on the ground.

The lionesses hunt in the early morning and in the evening when it is not so hot. After a big meal, you all have an extra-long sleep.

When you wake
up you have a
good, long stretch
and a big yawn.

You have a rough tongue covered in little spikes. When you lick your coat these spikes work like a brush and help to keep it clean. Your mother helps you keep your face clean.

You can clean all parts of your body except the top of your head

You rub heads together to say hello and to be friendly.

You live on your mother's milk for the first few months of your life.

You eat meat for the first time when you are about five months old.

Your mother and the other lionesses hunt for food. When they have killed an animal the male lions eat first, then the lionesses eat.

Finally, you eat with the other cubs. You do not chew your food. You tear off pieces of meat and swallow them whole.

You drink once a day,
early in the morning
or after eating at night.
You can go for many
days without a drink.

Sometimes you also go
for many days without
eating. When you are
old enough your mother
teaches you to hunt.

You learn to creep up on your prey through the long grass. You have to keep very quiet and still.

You pretend your mother's tail is an animal. You watch it waving and then pounce on it.

When you are a year old
you join your mother in
the hunt for food. You
follow her tail as a guide.

Your coat is a sandy
colour which helps
to hide you in the
long grass.

When you grow up you will have long, curved teeth and strong claws to help you catch your food.

If you are a male the hair on your head and neck will grow much longer and bushier.

By the time you are three years old you will have a beautiful mane of hair.

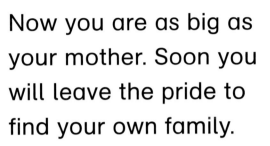

Now you are as big as your mother. Soon you will leave the pride to find your own family.

You are called the king of the beasts.

If you are a female, you
will have your first babies
when you are three or
four years old. You carry
the babies inside you
for about three months.

When they are ready to be born, you will leave the pride and look for somewhere safe for your cubs to be born.

You will look for a cave or the root of a tree. Both male and female lions live for about 20 years.

INDEX OF USEFUL WORDS

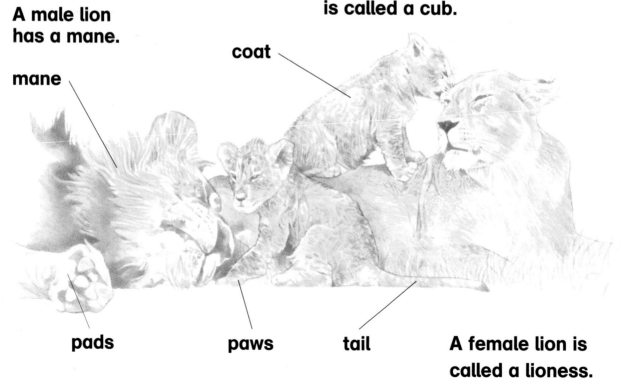

A male lion has a mane.

A baby lion is called a cub.

mane

coat

pads

paws

tail

A female lion is called a lioness.